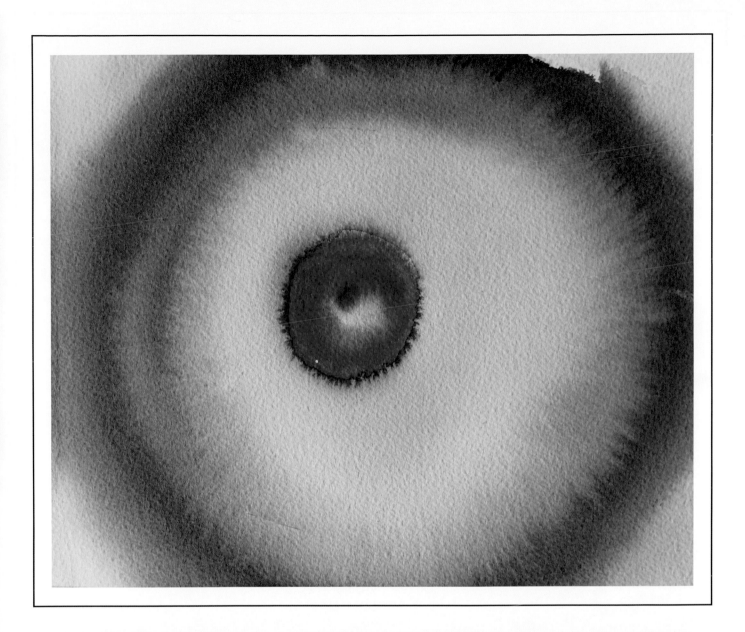

A
Warrior's
Simple Survival
Guide

Lou Lou Rose

Balboa Press books may be ordered through booksellers or by contacting:

Balboa Press
A Division of Hay House
1663 Liberty Drive
Bloomington, IN 47403
www.balboapress.com.au
1 (877) 407-4847

ISBN: 978-1-5043-1851-8 (sc)
ISBN: 978-1-5043-1852-5 (e)

Print information available on the last page.

Balboa Press rev. date: 11/15/2019

BALBOA
PRESS
A DIVISION OF HAY HOUSE

A

Warrior's

Simple Survival

Guide.

Dedication to our Fallen

Warriors.

To all of the Educators who have fallen or tripped, I dedicate this book to you.

Remembered Always

Nina Lampe. A women of immense grace and dignity. The most positive person I have ever had the good fortune to meet and work with. You are greatly missed.

Linda my predecessor who had hert11+ like me, but unfortunately no targeted therapy, like me.

Julie Field Another women of heart and passion who's journey was very brief. You are never forgotten. You always showed me great compassion.

Beth & Caroline

Also

Margaret Hagerty & Margaret O'Brien

Survivors

My Mum also a women with enormous grace, courage and bravery. My sister Anne-Marie. A true Warrior. Barbara Bradford you inspired me with your bravery, you truly have a heart of gold. Pat Lewis, a tri-athlete,I call the Survival Poster Girl. Nina Conti, Judith Willmott, Sally, Joe, Robyn, and every other Warrior who has fought the battle. I honor you all.

Contents

Diagnosis

There are many ways in which Cancer is first detected and the initial diagnosis will confirm or rule this out.

Further tests will be required in order to give a more accurate picture. Sometimes this may involve a biopsy, surgery or blood tests or a combination of the above.

We are fortunate in that we are now able to ascertain exactly what we have and therefore are able to treat the disease more successfully than ever before.

Unfortunately this cannot be rushed and it may take several weeks for them to be completed. This is the point in your life when you know you truly are on a different journey.

No one deserves to get cancer.

No one really knows why it happens

Maybe it's in our genes,

environmental or lifestyle.

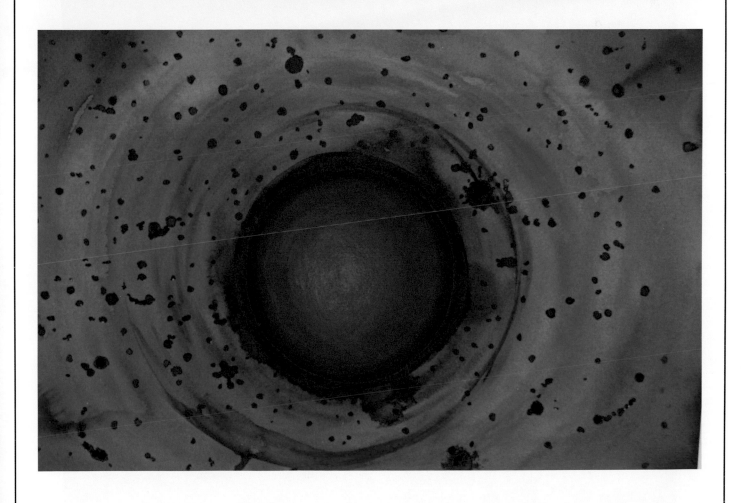

Diagnosis Continued

While you're waiting for your pathology results to return keep yourself busy with your work, family and/or friends.

This is a good time to seek out supportive company or take some time out if you'd prefer. Everyone reacts to things differently. While some people prefer to keep to themselves during challenging times in their lives, other people may prefer company.

I know quite a few medical professionals and I found them to be very supportive and informative. At this stage ensure you have access to one very good Doctor with whom you feel comfortable and who also has excellent Administrative Support.

Diagnosis Continued.

During this period of waiting I found going into nature very calming and relaxing.

When the time comes to receive your results whether in a private hospital or a public hospital, take someone with you if you can. But be mindful that you may wait up to three hours to see whichever Specialist is looking after you.

Take a distraction such as your phone or a good book. Most importantly take a good friend or a patient family member.

Don't ask people who are time poor as this can create more difficulties.

The reason this is called a journey, is because there are many stages of it and it may go on for some time.

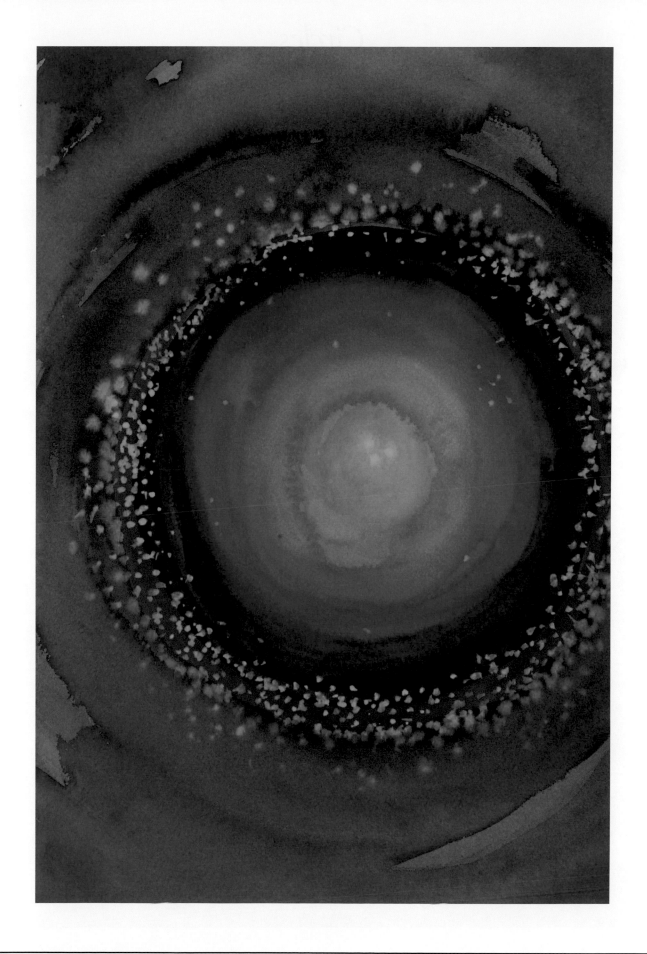

Circles

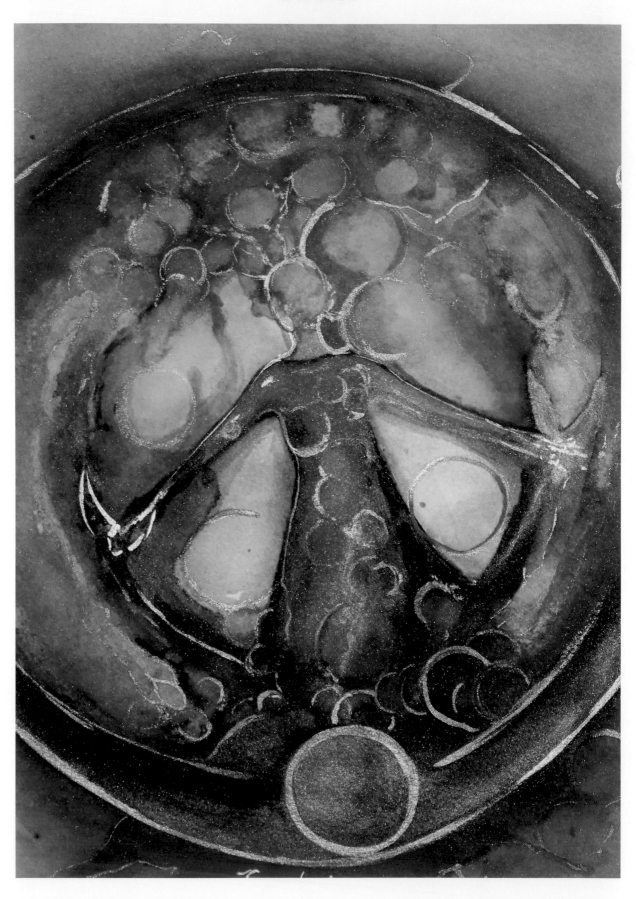

Circles

You may by now be feeling overwhelmed with the multitude of Specialist visits, information and other appointments you need to attend. The information not only needs to be understood but also shared.

This is where you may want to decide who will be in your inner circle. This circle should include people who genuinely care and make an attempt to understand your situation.

The people in this circle might be your immediate family members or very close friends.

These are the ones who need to know the current situation. It is wise to create a private group social Media page so you can easily relay what is happening without having to make multiple phone calls.

Circles cond.

It is also a good idea not to divulge too much information to people who you see day to day on a casual basis.

I know of a Warrior who went through this journey, and discussed diagnosis with everyone from the girl in the newsagency to all of her contacts on Face Book. This resulted in her being constantly reminded every time she went out to the newsagency. The cashier would tell her how many people she knew who either had cancer or had died from it recently.

Not what you need to hear on an outing to the shops. Actually telling someone this in this situation, is far from helpful.

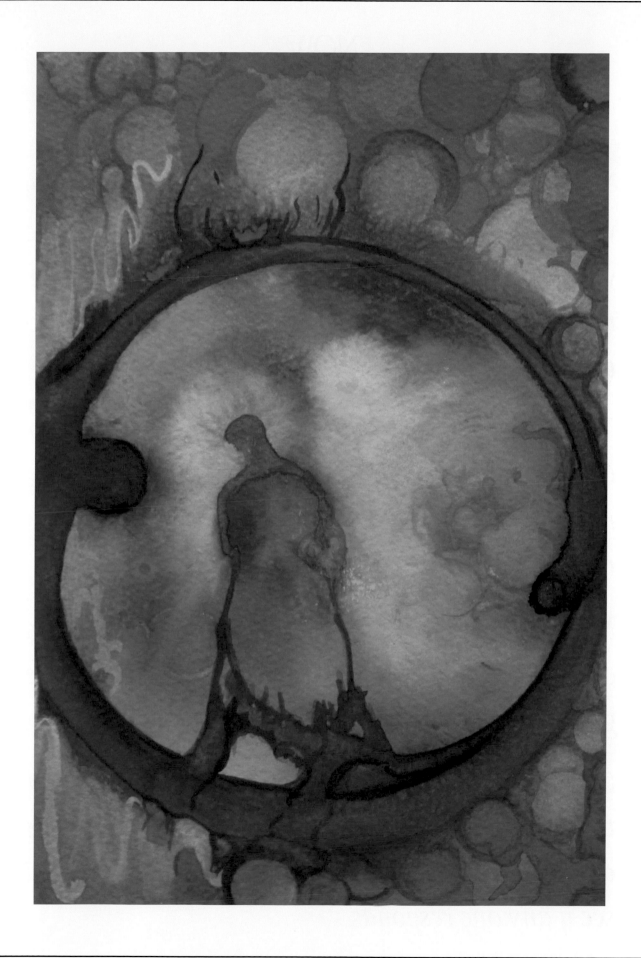

NOW
It really is all about YOU.

You may be some way into your treatment now which is great. It gives you a goal and a time frame with which to work. You will by now have met your multi-disciplinary team, who's main aim in life is to treat you and get you well again.

This may also be a time when you are at a low ebb. Going to and from medical appointments and having regular treatments, takes its toll. And sometimes the small things don't get done.

Maybe someone could help you with your shopping, or just drop off what you need. Church groups are great at this.

Or if you have a friend who loves to cook suggest that perhaps they could drop of a meal. Don't be afraid to ask. Or drop a hint on Social Media and see if any one responds.

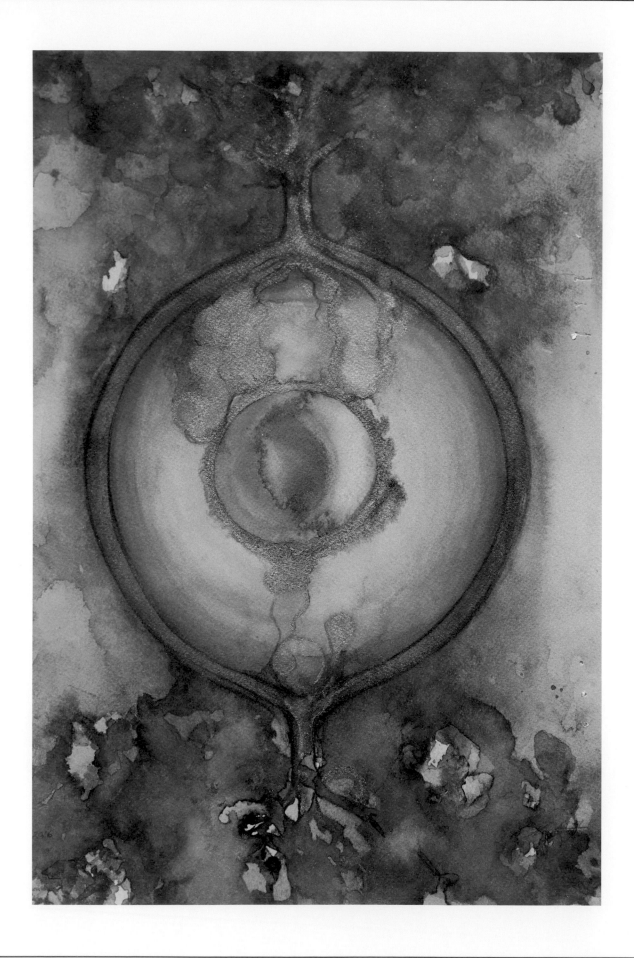

Just Be Positive.
"You just need to be positive."

A Warrior at this stage may have had surgery. they may have had Chemo and lost all of their beautiful hair. You don't know how important eye lashes are until you have none. (Use eye drops for the dryness and always wear sunglasses outside). And they may be feeling very overwhelmed. This can lead to fear, anger, confusion and if not handled adequately depression.

So please don't shut them down by telling them to just be positive. At this stage just being alive may be a major fete. Telling someone that they just need to be positive is dismissive and it closes down any communication they may have wanted to express to you.

They may relay a lot of information to you of which they are intimately knowlegable, but which you may find confusing. You can tell them that or, JUST LISTEN.

Let them rally and rave, this too will pass. Instead encourage them to get up (even if they feel they can't) and get them to go outside, like a good friend of mine once did. She didn't take no for an answer as I hadn't left my flat for days. So we went to the nearby park and walked and walk and walked. Until I was exhausted. (Which didn't take long). We collapsed in a heap on the grass and looked up at the stars. (Yes we went out at night) because she is a night owl. But it felt so good to feel the fresh cold air on my face and it was beautiful to see the stars. It was a moment I will never forget.

Looking after Yourself

Food has the potential to heal. So eat lots of fresh fruits, bright reds and oranges have heaps of anti-oxidents in them, as do legumes and oats. If you're not really into fruit, juices are a good substitute.

I walked most days during my treatment, and on days when I wasn't feeling particularly great, I'd choose a place where I was close to medical attention. Parks next to Hospitals are a great choice, shopping centers are great, especially in hot or inclement weather.

If you are feeling strong enough a walk by the ocean can do wonders for both your body and mind. I benefited greatly from soaking myself in the ocean. The ocean is like natures anti-inflammatory. I always swam were a life guard was vigilant. If you like trees find a quiet place in your park and listen to the birds and smell the clean fresh air.

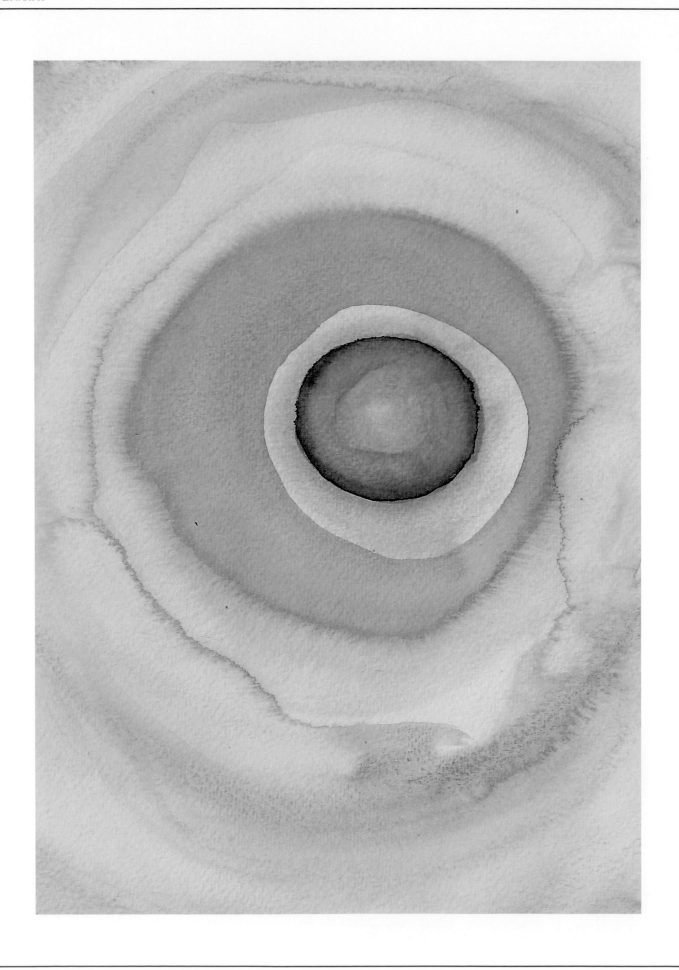

Looking after Yourself Check List.

1. Before surgery (if you need to have it) stop drinking alcohol. This will greatly reduce your recovery time.

2. Replenish your reserves with good wholesome foods. Try making a beef broth.

3. When having chemo, drink lots and lots and lots of water.

4. Soak in a nice Epsom salts bath. If the ocean isn't possible.

5. Cut your hair short, if you're having chemo.

6. Keep your finger nails short also.

7. Wear sun block always.

8. Use moisture drops for your eyes & wear sunglasses.

9. Stay away from chemicals, both beauty & houseold.

10. Bonjella is great for mouth ulcers.

11. For radiation therapy use plenty of Moo Goo or naturally based moisturizers.

12. Try to keep moving.

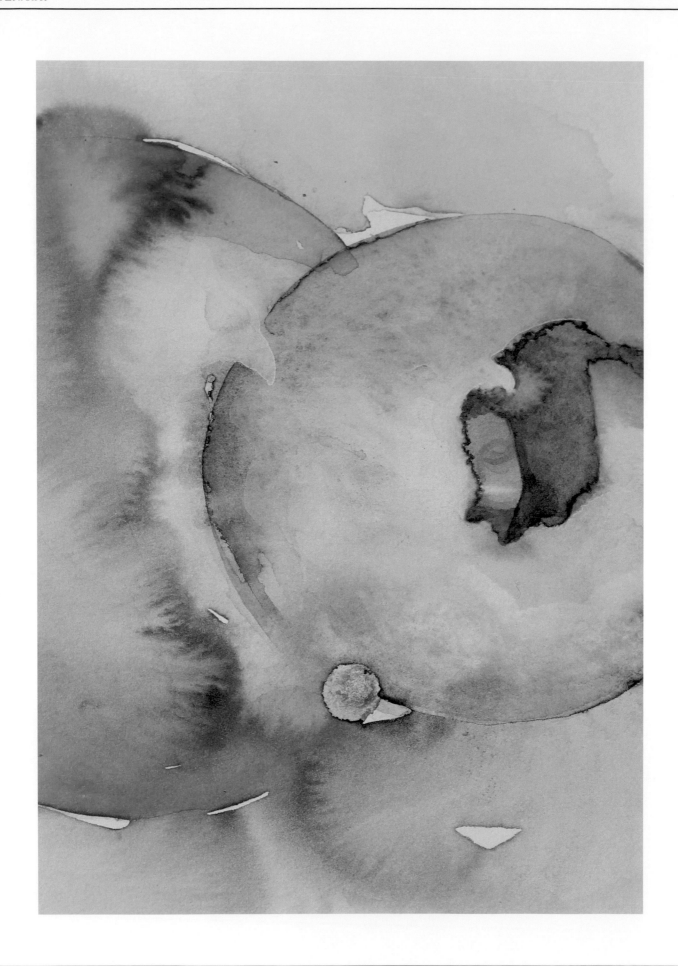

Warrior Spirit.

If your beautiful friend has had Chemotherapy or Targeted Therapy, this is the time they will truly become a Warrior.

This is also a time when a friend can really step up and help out. You might be able to attend an appointment with them. It's always good to have another person present when there is a lot of waiting around.

It's also very important to have another person to drive or to pick up our warrior after treatments.

They don't necessarily need someone to stay. Just drop them off or pick them up or both if time permits.

If this kind of assistance is unavailable from a friend, many hospitals have shuttle buses to and from stations. Some have patient transportation, for those who really need to be picked up from home.

Reclaiming Your Own Power

Unfortunately some people lose their sense of power when going through this situation. They have their multi-disciplinary team and also hospital protocols which must be followed. This can lead to a feeling of disempowerment.

Do your research and listen to what the Professionals are advising you to do. They do know what they are talking about. If you're not happy seek a second opinion. Do try to stay away from Dr. Google if you can as it is often misleading and unhelpful. Much better to access a group site comprised of people just like yourself as well as medical professionals.

Relay your concerns to your team and together make a choice or choices with which you feel you own and are comfortable with

Consult with the Nurse Liasion Officer who is trained to guide and steer you in the right direction and often times are more approachable and accessible then the specialist.

Learn to say no if you are not comfortable with something.

If you find this difficult seek professional guidance from a Psychologist.

They can easily teach you strategies to make this easier.

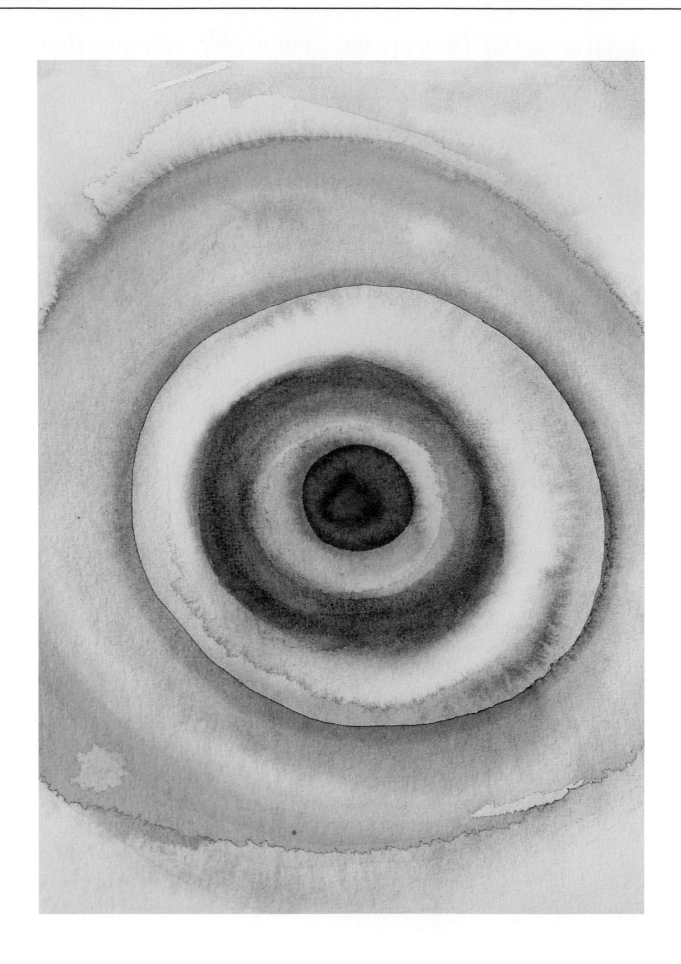

Learn to Smile and Laugh Again.

This is a tool all good Oncologists use. My own Oncologist used it every time I visited him.

My homework was to find a joke I could tell him. We both set parameters for their suitability. They couldn't be about death or illness of course. They were not allowed to be racist or sexist or cruel or too rude. As you can imagine the pool wasn't very big. So this kept me busy for weeks and weeks.

We would start each consultation with one of our terrible jokes. And the worse they were the more we would laugh. In fact I knew when I'd told a good one because he would sit there leaned in towards me listening intently, trying hard to remember, because I just knew he'd relay it to someone else later. Or so I'd like to believe. This tactic was double fold because he'd often tell me the same one twice. I think in order to gauge how my memory was. As I'd let him know if he'd told me he same joke more than once. Either way we both had fun.

Do What You Love.

It's important to still feel connected to society if you are not yet back at work. Join a Survivors Gym and meet people who can understand what you are going through. Get fit along the way and make some new friends. You will lose some along this journey. But you'll also find out who your true friends are.

Or if you'd like to try something more creative there are a multitude of workshops both online and as meet ups. I personally would rather do one's unrelated to the Hosp. as there were already too many visits there. Find a place in which you feel comfortable. And try to attend as often as possible. If money is an issue the Hosp. run workshops are free and you may be able to go to another hospital.

Knitting can be very relaxing if you're into that sort of thing. It is a great way to keep your mind occupied and you will end up with a garment to wear or give away.

If you feel ready to return to work and it is something you love to do. Do it. But remember the Circle's. It still holds here as well, and not everyone needs to know everything.

Audley Boat House

Transformation

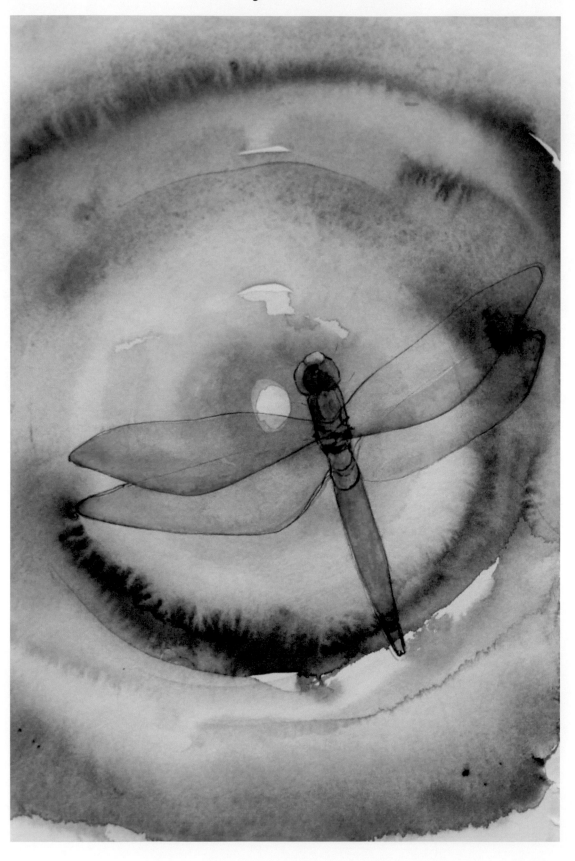

New Journey

So you've made it through

Reward yourself.

You deserve it.

If you can afford to, go on that holiday you've always wanted to go on. If you can't, start planning it.

Spend time with the people you love and really be present with them. They are probably the few who made it from beginning to end with you.

Nurture yourself with good food, good company and exercise, meditation & yoga. Sing, dance, draw, paint or learn to play a musical instrument.

What ever made you truly happy.

Do what you love to do as often as you can. But above all else; (as my Oncologist said).

It's time to start concentrating on really living again.

How are you Travelling Today?

....

....

....

....

....

....

....

....

....

....

....

....

....

....

....

....

....

What is on your Mind?

··

··

··

··

··

··

··

··

··

··

··

··

··

··

··

··

··

··

Clarify what you mean & say it.

(What do you need to say & to whom to you need to say it?)

....

....

....

....

....

Make time for creating.

This can be something as simple as a prayer shawl, a favourite meal or a beautiful painting. It's up to you. Note down a few ideas.

....

....

....

....

....

Honor those you Love.

Nurture your

Mind, body & Soul.

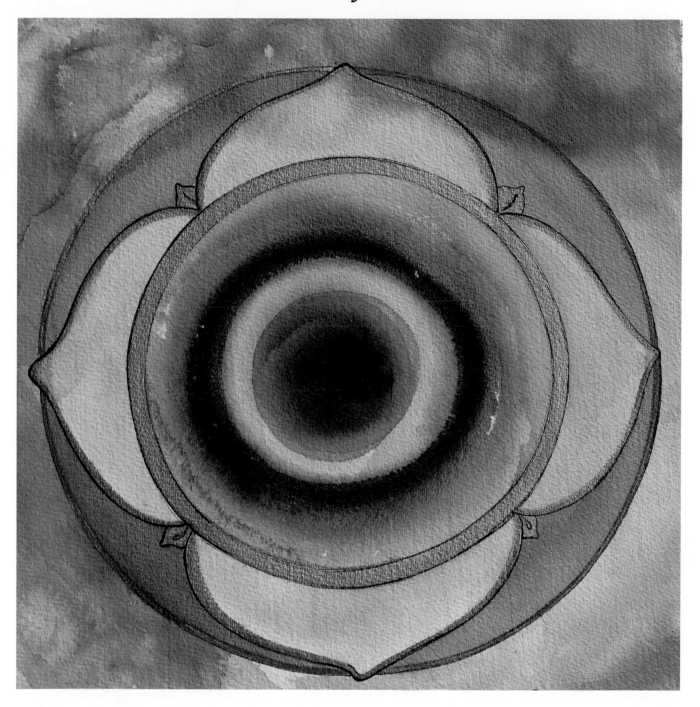

Time to Heal & Love Yourself

....

....

....

....

....

....

....

....

....

....

....

....

....

....

....

....

....

....

....

....

....

Once Treatment is Over.

While you are going through treatment you will be in fight and flight mode. This takes a lot of energy and isn't good for you long term.

Those people with good intentions who told you to just be positive, had a point. Which is the mind is a very powerful tool, and it has the potential to heal the body if you let it. Now is the time to start to look at yourself wholistically.

Throughout this book I have outlined what helped me personally. But an Author who studied hundreds of stage four cancer warriors came up with the following eight life altering changes, which saw them overcome and survive cancer. They are:

Radically Change Your Diet

Take Control of Your Health

Follow Your Intuition

Release Suppressed Emotions

Increase Positive Emotions

Embrace Social Support

Deepen Your Spiritual Connection

Have a Strong Life Purpose

I send you love

&

Wish you Well

On Your

Journey.

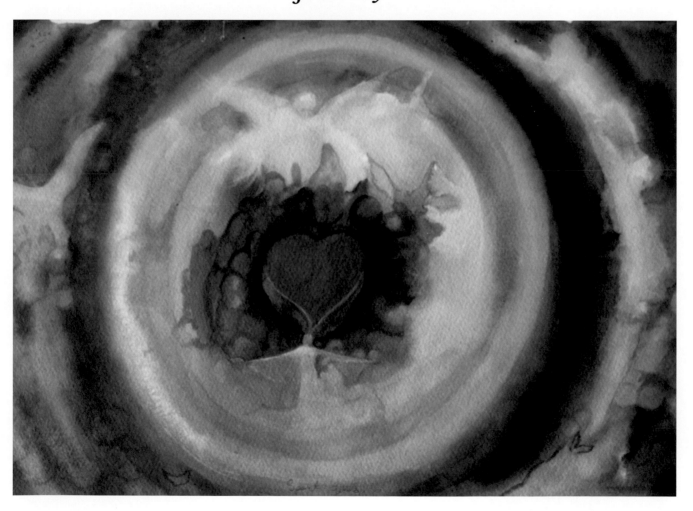

Printed in the United States
By Bookmasters